MOUNT RUSHMORE

Amy Culliford

TABLE OF CONTENTS

A Pelican Book

Teaching Tips for Caregivers and Teachers:

Research shows that one of the best ways for students to learn a new topic is to read about it.

Before Reading

- Read the title and predict what the book will be about.
- Read the "Words to Know" and discuss the meaning of each word.
- Read the back cover to see what the book is about.

During Reading

- When a student gets to a word that is unknown, ask them to look at the rest of the sentence to find clues to help with the meaning of the unknown word.
- Motivate students with praise and encouragement.

After Reading

- Discuss the main idea of the book.
- Ask students to give one detail that they learned in the book.

Sight Words

a
American
are
day
every
faces
four
go
I
in
is
it
made
many
of
on
people
see
the
to
was
with

Words to Know

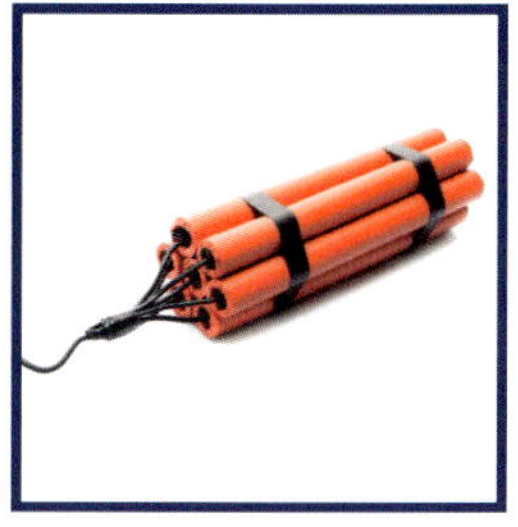

dynamite

Mount Rushmore

mountain

Presidents

South Dakota

I see **Mount Rushmore**!

Mount Rushmore

Mount Rushmore is in
South Dakota.

UNITED STATES OF AMERICA

It is on a **mountain**.

mountain

It was made with **dynamite**.

The faces are of four American **Presidents**.

Presidents

Many people go to see Mount Rushmore every day!

Written by: Amy Culliford
Design by: Under the Oaks Media
Series Development: James Earley
Editor: Kim Thompson

Photos: John D Smith: cover; Shu-Hung Liu: p. 4-5; TD Dolci: p. 9; Nomad_Soul: p. 10; Everett Collection: p. 11; Galyna Andrushko: p. 13; photo.ua: p. 15

Library of Congress PCN Data
Mount Rushmore / Amy Culliford
U.S. Landmarks
ISBN 978-1-63897-075-0 (hard cover)
ISBN 978-1-63897-161-0 (paperback)
ISBN 978-1-63897-247-1 (EPUB)
ISBN 978-1-63897-333-1 (eBook)
Library of Congress Control Number: 2021945231

Printed in the United States of America.

Seahorse Publishing Company
www.seahorsepub.com

Published in the United States
Seahorse Publishing
PO Box 771325
Coral Springs, FL 33077